twilight
the score

ISBN 978-1-4234-7467-8

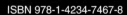

HAL•LEONARD®
CORPORATION
7777 W. BLUEMOUND RD. P.O. BOX 13819 MILWAUKEE, WI 53213

In Australia Contact:
Hal Leonard Australia Pty. Ltd.
4 Lentara Court
Cheltenham, Victoria, 3192 Australia
Email: ausadmin@halleonard.com.au

Visit Hal Leonard Online at
www.halleonard.com

edward

twilight

james

twilight

WHO ARE THEY?

Composed by
CARTER BURWELL

Moderately fast

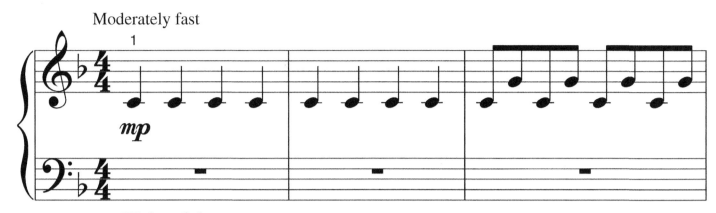

With pedal

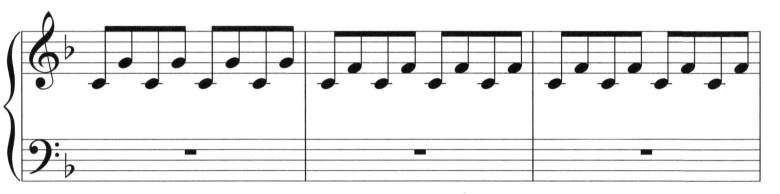

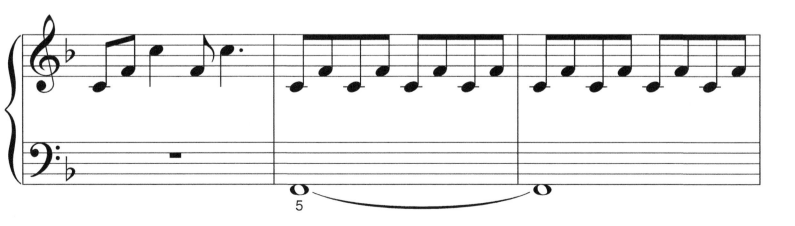

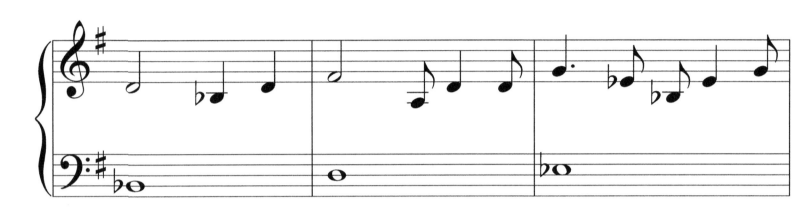

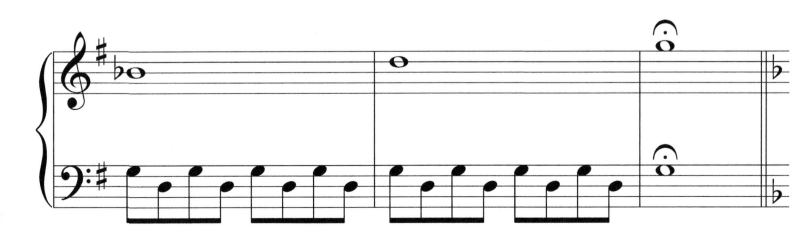

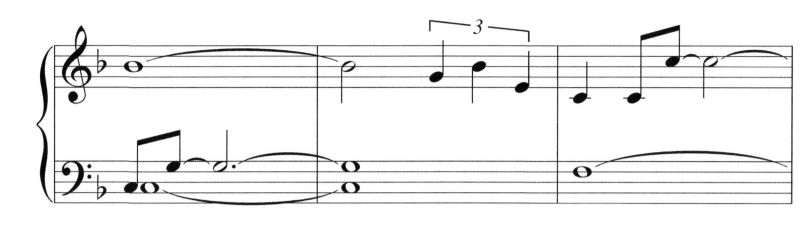

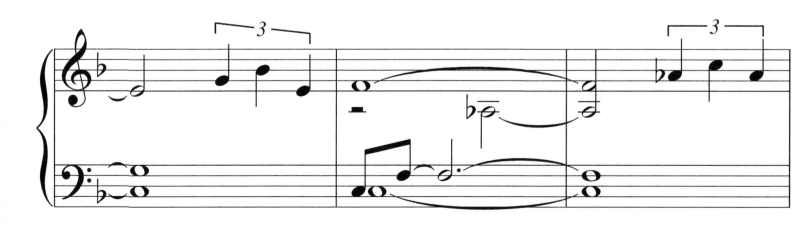

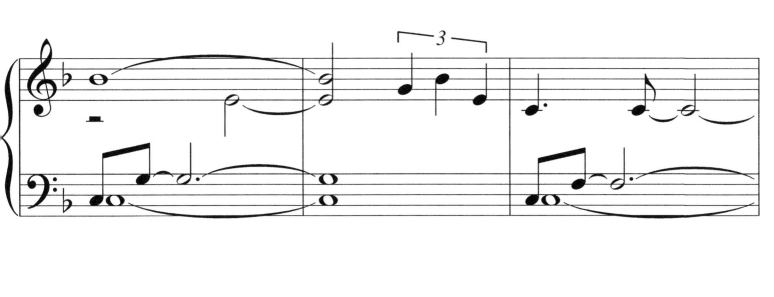

Slightly slower

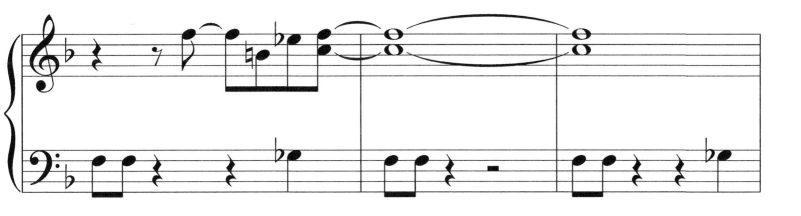

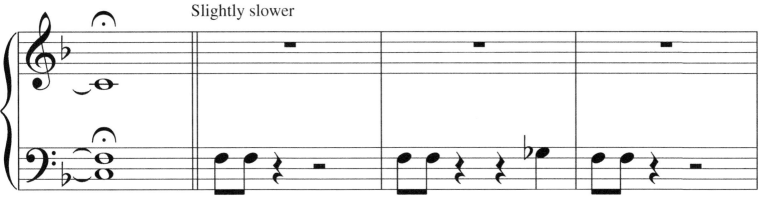

PHASCINATION PHASE

Composed by
CARTER BURWELL

Moderately slow, in 2

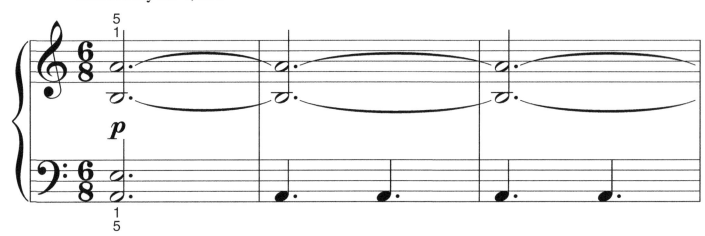

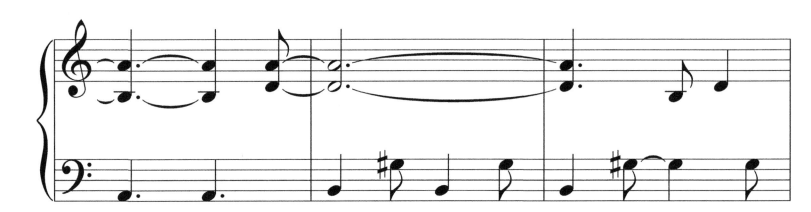

I DREAMT OF EDWARD

Composed by
CARTER BURWELL

Moderately slow

THE LION FELL IN LOVE
WITH THE LAMB

Composed by
CARTER BURWELL

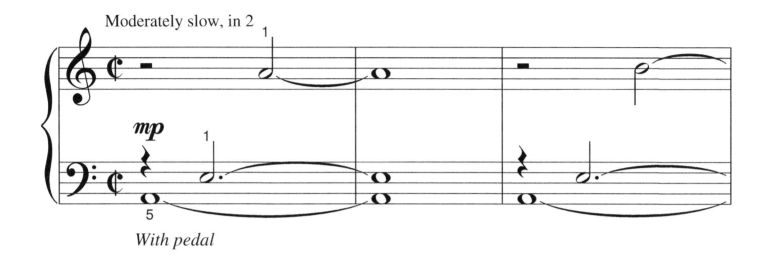

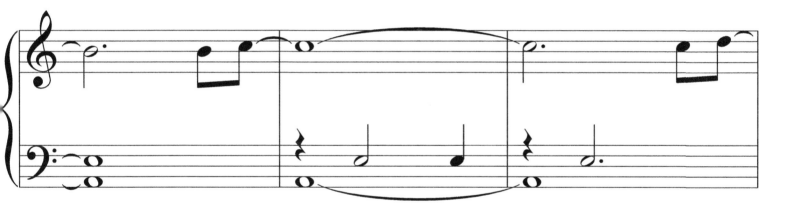

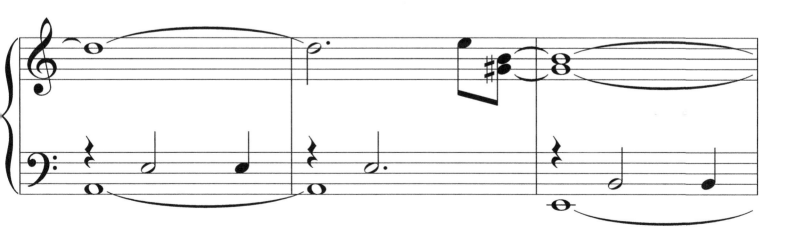

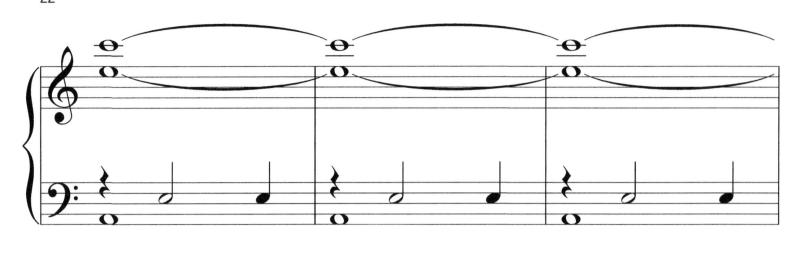

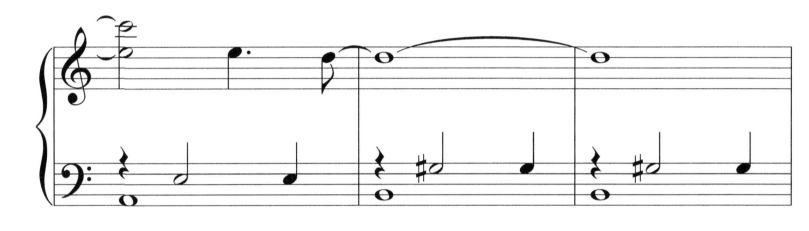

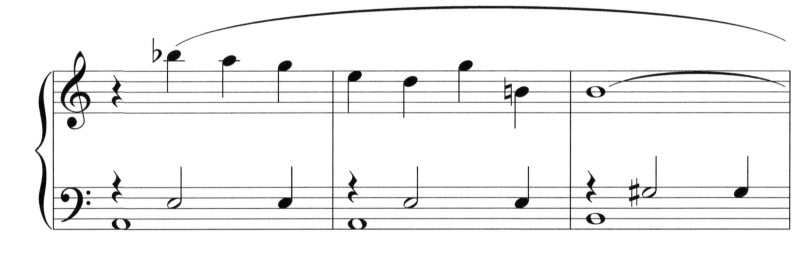

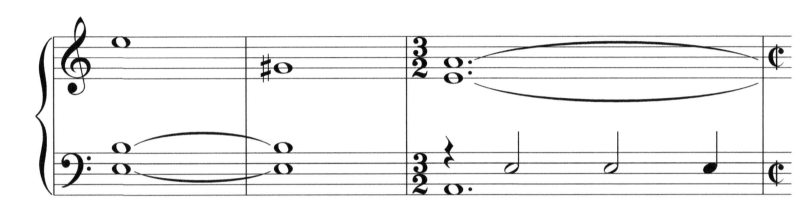

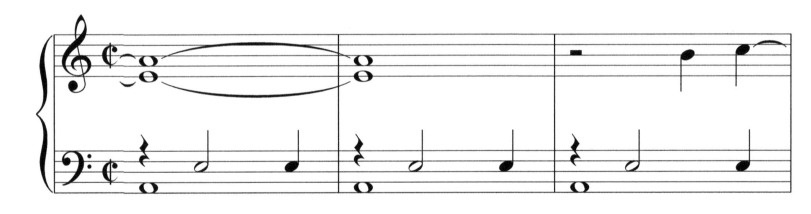

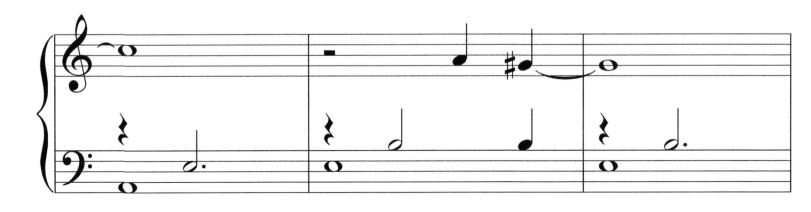

DINNER WITH HIS FAMILY

Composed by
CARTER BURWELL

STUCK HERE LIKE MOM

Composed by
CARTER BURWELL

Moderately

With pedal

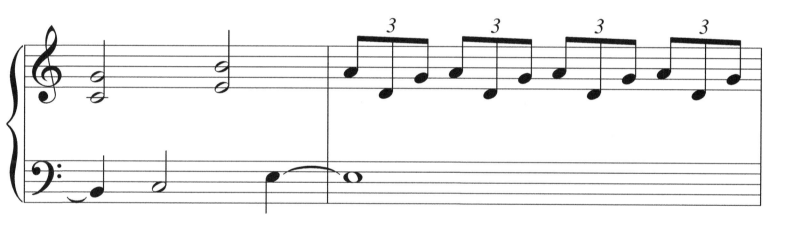

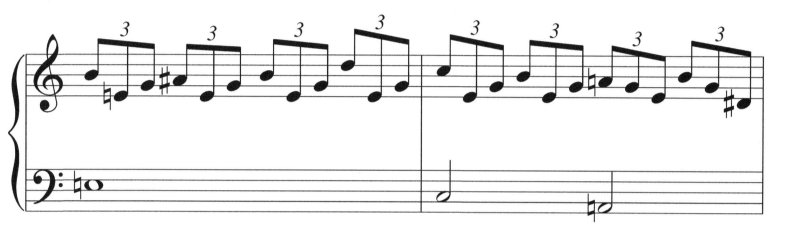

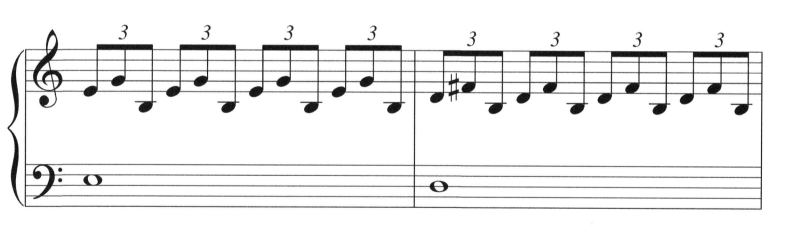

I WOULD BE THE MEAL

Composed by
CARTER BURWELL

BELLA'S LULLABY

Composed by
CARTER BURWELL

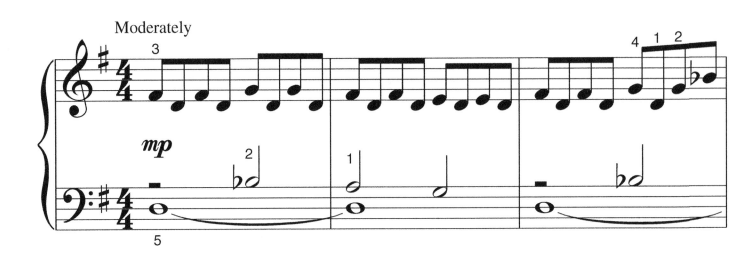

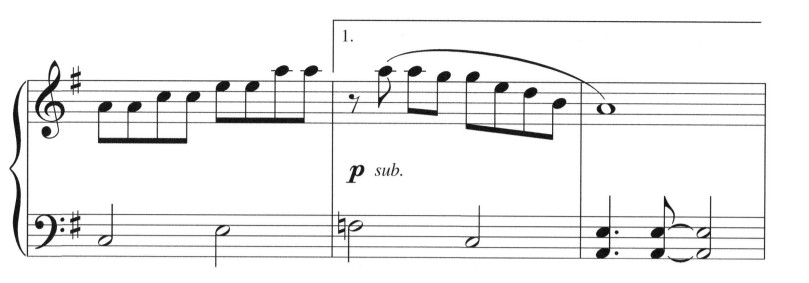

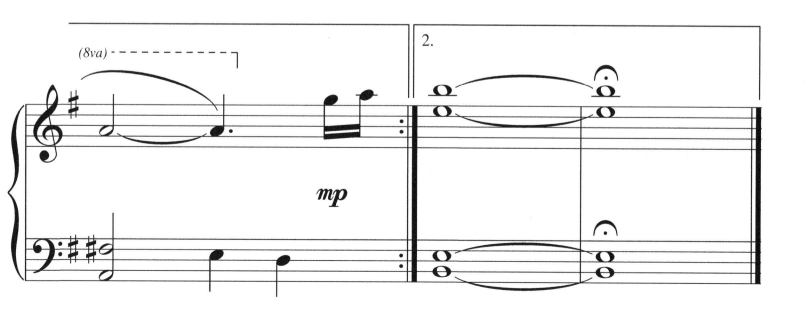

TRACKING

Composed by
CARTER BURWELL

Slowly, in 2

With pedal

EDWARD AT HER BED

Composed by
CARTER BURWELL

IN PLACE OF SOMEONE YOU LOVE

Composed by
CARTER BURWELL

Moderately

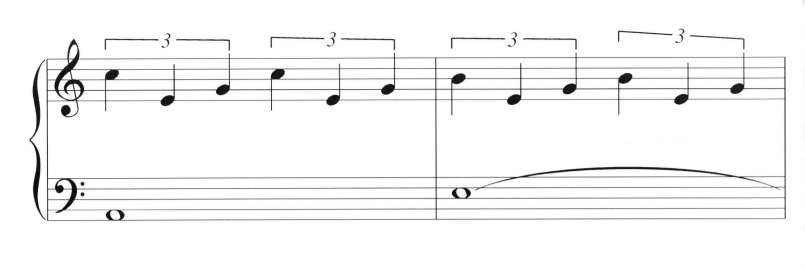

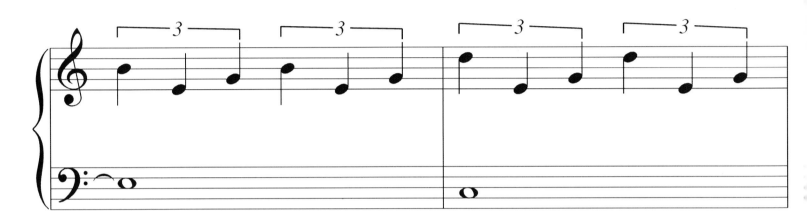

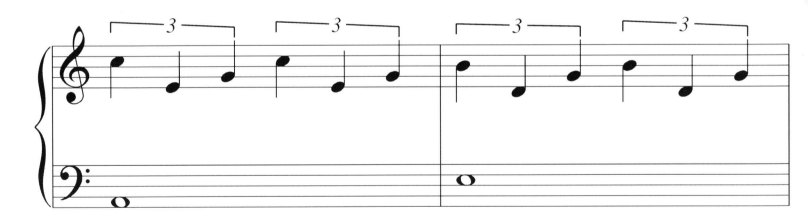

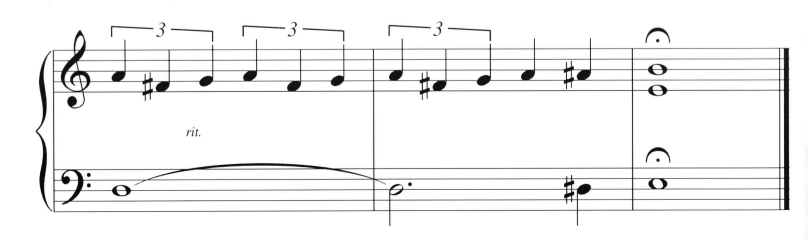